# THE WONDERFUL WORLD OF WORDS

**9**

## The King Helps Mr Anteater

## Dr Lubna Alsagoff

PhD Linguistics (Stanford)

**Marshall Cavendish**
Children

One morning, King Norman Nautilus Noun was walking in the beautiful garden of WOW.

He saw Mr Anteater sitting sadly on a log.

What's wrong, Mr Anteater?

No matter how hard I try, I cannot catch enough ants to eat!

The plurals flew into the air and landed on all the nouns that were more than one.

one ant

two ant s

three ant s

four ant s

Mr Anteater could count once more!
What a lovely meal of ants he had!

Mr Anteater was very happy. Finally, he could eat his lunch. So he poked his long snout once more into the log and began to eat.

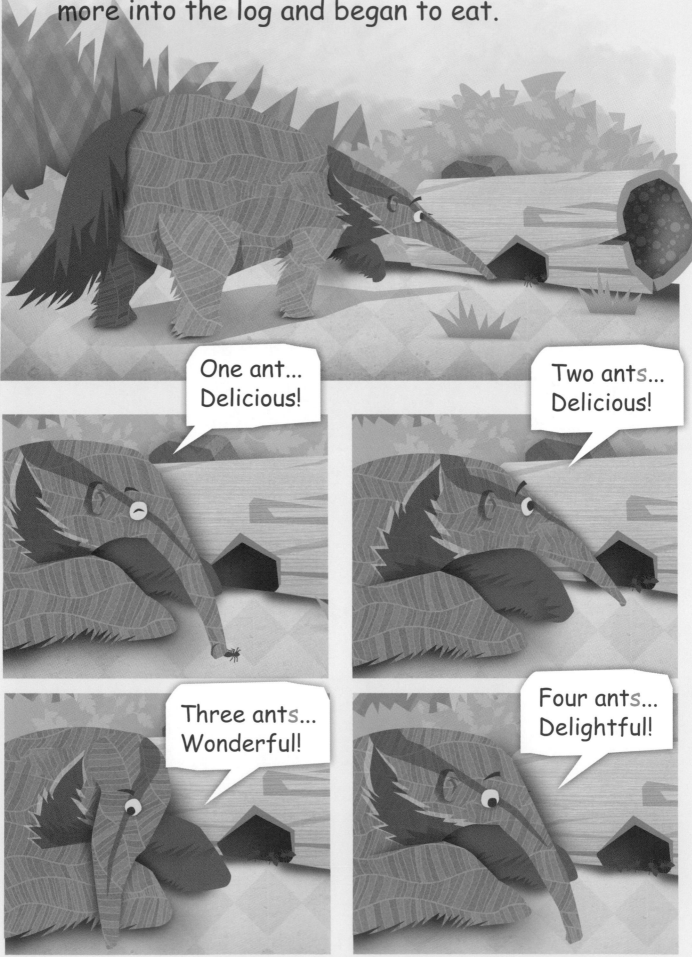

One ant... Delicious!

Two ants... Delicious!

Three ants... Wonderful!

Four ants... Delightful!

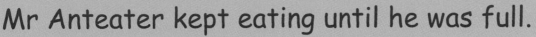

Mr Anteater kept eating until he was full.

I have eaten so many ants, thanks to the perfectly pretty plurals!

Mr Anteater was now very happy but Mrs Fox was not happy at all.

King Noun, what about my little foxes?

Some foxes love buses.

Some can sew with fine stitches.

Others love blowing kisses...

...to foxes hiding behind bushes!

Mrs Fox was right.

King Noun pulled out more plurals. These were different.

Yes indeed, Mrs Fox!

⭐ We add **es** to make the plural for nouns ending with x, s, sh, and ch.

Your little foxes need different plurals.

| fox | + | es | → | foxes |
| bus | + | es | → | buses |
| stitch | + | es | → | stitches |
| kiss | + | es | → | kisses |
| bush | + | es | → | bushes |

Some nouns that end with o take an **s**, and some take an **es**:

| | | |
|---|---|---|
| piano | → | pianos |
| radio | → | radios |
| hero | → | heroes |
| potato | → | potatoes |

And even when they have **s** or **es** plurals, some nouns need special rules!

Nouns that end with **f** or **fe** change the f to a **v** with the plural **es**:

| | | |
|---|---|---|
| loaf | → | loaves |
| elf | → | elves |
| knife | → | knives |

Nouns that end with a consonant (a sound that is not a vowel) and a **y** have to change the y to an **i** with the plural **es**:

| | | |
|---|---|---|
| baby | → | babies |
| city | → | cities |
| lady | → | ladies |

The king also knew that there were nouns in WOW which did not even want perfectly pretty *s* or *es* plurals.

One **foot**

Many **feet**

One **person**

Many **people**

Mrs Mouse and Mrs Goose didn't need the *s* or *es* plurals! Mrs Mouse liked her little mice. And Mrs Goose loved the other geese!

One m**ouse**

Many **mice**

One **goose**

Many **geese**

Mrs Sheep and Mr Deer did not seem to need plurals at all!

One **sheep**

Many **sheep**

One **deer**

Many **deer**

11

ants

ant

When a noun names more than one thing, it is plural.

When a noun names one thing, it is singular.

Remember the rules!

- You make a plural by adding **s** at the end of the noun.

- Nouns that end with x, s, sh or ch have special plurals. You add **es** to make these nouns plural.

- Some nouns change their spelling. So, an f becomes v, and y becomes i for some nouns.

- Some nouns don't change even when they are plural.

# What kind of plurals do these nouns have?

| SINGULAR | PLURAL |
|----------|--------|
| leg | |
| atlas | |
| army | |
| wish | |
| guitar | |
| tax | |
| sandwich | |
| cherry | |
| hoof | |
| sketch | |
| half | |
| class | |

Can you help the perfectly pretty plurals look for the regular nouns they can be with? Join the dots and find the star!

monkey

moose

watch

bus

deer

stitch

picture

bag

antelope

cup

house

gorilla

shoe

door

toy

sock

child

cousin

knife

badge

goat

torch

goose

tooth

tongue

table

boat

tiger

light

oyster

son

mouse

wife

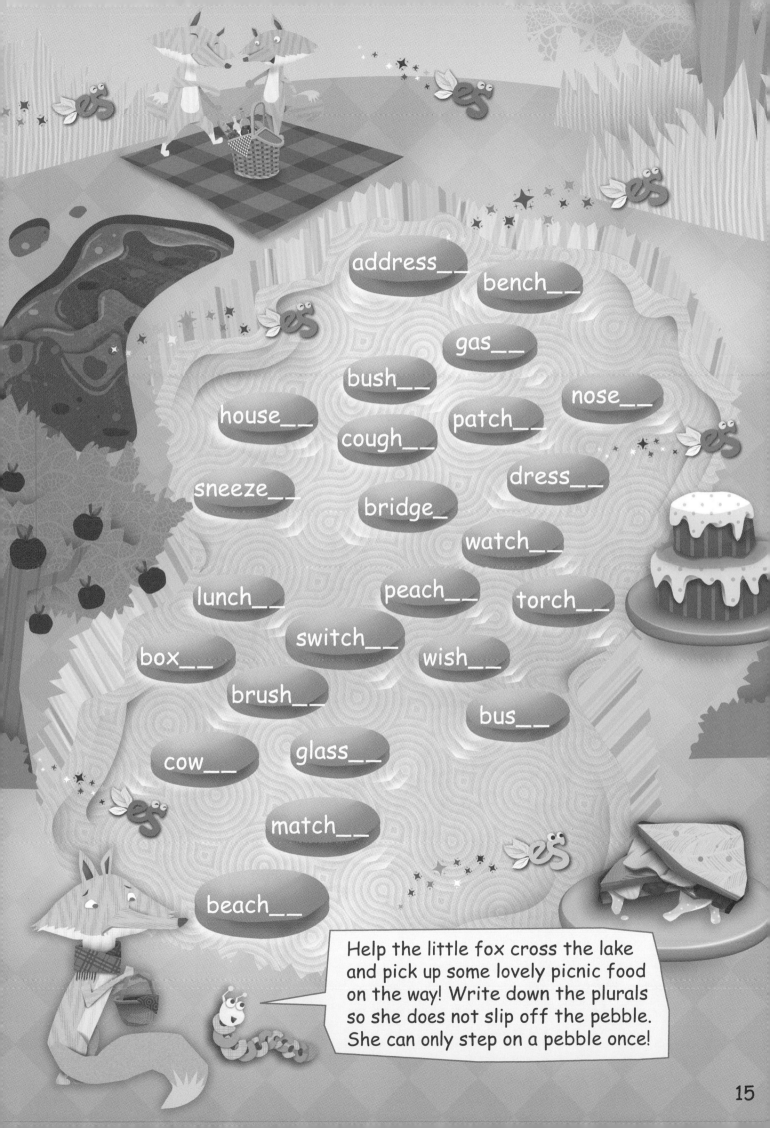

address__

bench__

gas__

bush__

nose__

house__

patch__

cough__

dress__

sneeze__

bridge_

watch__

lunch__

peach__

torch__

switch__

wish__

box__

brush__

bus__

cow__

glass__

match__

beach__

Help the little fox cross the lake and pick up some lovely picnic food on the way! Write down the plurals so she does not slip off the pebble. She can only step on a pebble once!

Magpie was worried the princess would get angry with her.

She decided to take the princess to see Owl, Rabbit and Squirrel.

Princess, you must be tired and hungry! Why don't we go and meet my friends?

Oh, that would be nice. I am hungry after my long journey from the castle.

Soon, Magpie and the princess arrive at Donkey's house.

They hear strange sounds coming from the house.

Donkey hears Magpie squawking outside his home.

Donkey, may we come in?

Hello, Donkey. My name is Princess Preposition.

Hello, Princess. Would you like to come in to have **HICCUP** cup a of tea and **HICCUP** biscuit some?

Can you help Donkey to say things the right way?

22

Princess Preposition knew something was wrong with Donkey. She wondered what had happened to him.

Dear Parents,

In this issue, children should notice and learn:

- The different plurals that nouns have.
- The rules that are used to spell these plurals.
- That some plural nouns look the same as the singular nouns.

| Page | Possible Answers |
|---|---|
| 13 | legs \| atlases \| armies \| wishes \| guitars \| taxes \| sandwiches \| cherries \| hooves \| sketches \| halves \| classes |
| 14 | |

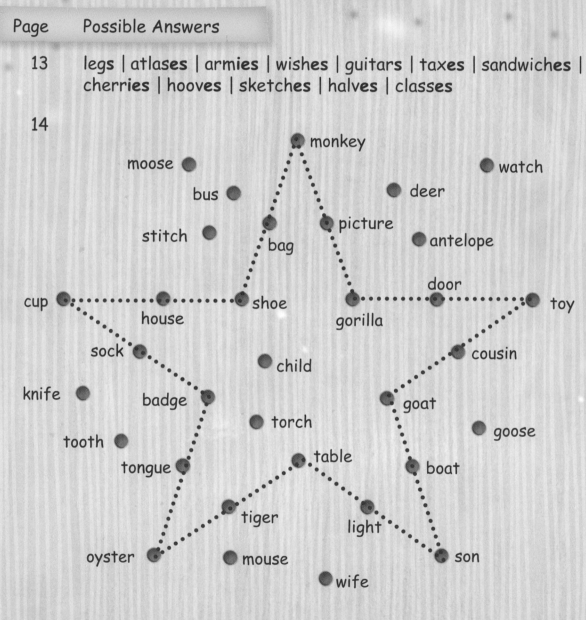

| 15 | beaches \| matches \| glasses \| brushes \| boxes \| lunches \| switches \| peaches \| wishes \| buses \| torches \| watches \| dresses \| patches \| bushes \| gases \| benches \| addresses |